A Drop In The Bucket

_____

Name

_____

Date

Wine to Water Project

To: _____

A Drop In The Bucket is your personal journal. Here you will transfer your thoughts, feelings, ideas and dreams into words.

A Drop In The Bucket

Copyright © 2014

ISBN: 978-1-935256-39-7

Ledge Press
PO Box 1652
Boone, NC 28607
www.ledgepress.com
ledgepress@gmail.com

Why?

The culture we live in leaves us little room for "quietness," but we all need to seek time to be alone and "get away from the crowds." Today's crowds are not like they were 2000 years ago. Our lives are crowded by constant noise. The noise of technology. TV, Facebook, emails, Twitter, texting, etc. Technology is neutral. It is neither bad nor good. It just is.

But think about a typical day. Think about the interactions of a day. The people. The computer. The phone. The "messages." Crowded.

Ahead is an adventure, a journey. It may be your first volunteer project or it could be one of several. This little journal was made to enhance your experience. To deepen the adventure. To interact with yourself and others. We will dive into the physical world and its issues. We want also to dive into the spiritual world and see how physical water meets needs and how spiritual water can also meet needs.

Over the next few weeks, take time to reflect on your upcoming adventure. During your experience take time to reflect and record what is on your heart and mind. And when you return home from your adventure, journal the aftermath.

Sneak away from the "crowds" of your life and find a place, to be alone. And interact with your adventure. Pen your thoughts. Record your reflections.

There are three stages to this journal, which reflects the three stages of your upcoming adventure.

The first stage is Preparation or pre-Adventure. During this stage you will be meeting with your team. Preparing for the volunteer experience. Learning about the country and the people you will be serving. Ten to twelve days prior to your volunteer trip, pull out your journal and begin to prepare your heart and mind. Listen. Read. Think. Pray. Record.

The second stage is the actual project or the Adventure. It launches when your feet touch the ground in your host country. This will be an exciting and busy time. You will be "crowded" and your daily schedule filled with new experiences. This is the time you will have to be intentional with finding a time to slip away and be alone. During this time: Listen. Read. Think. Pray. Record.

The third stage is the post-Adventure. It begins when your feet touch the ground in your home country. There will be memories. Enthusiasm from what you have just experienced. A gradual return to your normal routine. You will go through shifting emotions and begin to merge your recent Adventure with the normal routines of being home. This is a critical time to capture what is passing through your mind and heart. During this stage: Listen. Read. Think. Pray. Record.

Date: _____   Word: Dirt

Reading: The Lord God formed man of dust from the ground and breathed into his nostrils the breath of life; and man became a living being. Genesis 2:7

What other words come to mind with this word:
Dirty. Clean. Garden. Plants. Food. Seeds. Fruit.

This page is a "Sample Page."

Each Journal page will have a place to record the day/ date.

At the top of each page of your journal will be a "word." This word will be your guide for that day. It will lead you down a path for you to think and pray about what that word means for you during that particular part of your Adventure.

A passage or quote is listed which corresponds to the particular word for that day.

And finally, the rest of the page is yours to explore your thoughts, dreams, ideas and prayers.

_____

_____

_____

_____

_____

Date: _____ Word: Build

Reading: Yet it is in the whole process of meeting and solving problems that our life has its meaning. Problems are the cutting edge that distinguishes between success and failure. Problems call forth our courage and our wisdom; indeed, they create our courage and wisdom. It is only because of problems that we grow mentally and spiritually. Scott M. Peck

What other words come to mind with this word:

_____

_____

_____

_____

_____

_____

_____

_____

_____

_____

_____

_____

_____

_____

_____

_____

_____

_____

_____

Date: _____ Word: Quest

Reading: Anyone who doesn't take truth seriously in small matters cannot be trusted in large ones either. Einstein

Walk with the wise and become wise, for a companion of fools suffers harm. Proverbs 13:20

What other words come to mind with this word:

_____
_____
_____
_____
_____
_____
_____
_____
_____
_____
_____
_____
_____
_____
_____
_____
_____
_____
_____
_____

Date: _____ Word: Hearing

Reading: When the solution is simple, God is answering. Einstein

Those who guard their mouths and their tongues keep themselves from calamity. Proverbs 21:23

What other words come to mind with this word:

_____
_____
_____
_____
_____
_____
_____
_____
_____
_____
_____
_____
_____
_____
_____
_____
_____
_____
_____
_____
_____
_____

Date: _____ Word: Physical

Reading: I have a new philosophy. I'm only going to dread one day at a time.
Charles M. Schulz

What other words come to mind with this word:

_____
_____
_____
_____
_____
_____
_____
_____
_____
_____
_____
_____
_____
_____
_____
_____
_____
_____
_____
_____
_____
_____

Date: _____ Word: Real

Reading: In the beginning God created the heavens and the earth. Genesis 1:1

Those who guard their lips preserve their lives, but those who speak rashly come to ruin. Proverbs 13:3

What other words come to mind with this word:

_____
_____
_____
_____
_____
_____
_____
_____
_____
_____
_____
_____
_____
_____
_____
_____
_____
_____
_____
_____
_____

Date: _____ Word: Intentional

Reading: The difference between what we do and what we are capable of doing would suffice to solve most of the world's problem. Gandhi

What other words come to mind with this word:

_____

_____

_____

_____

_____

_____

_____

_____

_____

_____

_____

_____

_____

_____

_____

_____

_____

_____

_____

_____

_____

_____

_____

Date: _____ Word: Prepared

Reading: Whatever you do may seem insignificant to you, but it is most important that you do it. Gandhi

What other words come to mind with this word:

_____

_____

_____

_____

_____

_____

_____

_____

_____

_____

_____

_____

_____

_____

_____

_____

_____

_____

_____

_____

_____

_____

_____

Date: _____ Word: Rain

Reading: Our lives begin to end the day we become silent about the things that matter. Martin Luther King, Jr.

What other words come to mind with this word:

_____
_____
_____
_____
_____
_____
_____
_____
_____
_____
_____
_____
_____
_____
_____
_____
_____
_____
_____
_____
_____
_____
_____
_____

Date: _____ Word: World

Reading: Being heard is so close to being loved that for the average person they are almost indistinguishable. To say something you value deeply to another and to have him or her value it equally by listening to it carefully and appreciatively is the most universal way of exchanging social interest and demonstrating affection. David Augusburger

What other words come to mind with this word:

_____
_____
_____
_____
_____
_____
_____
_____
_____
_____
_____
_____
_____
_____
_____
_____
_____
_____

Date: _____ Word: Wait

Reading: If it's your job to eat a frog, it's best to do it first thing in the morning. And if it's your job to eat two frogs, it's best to eat the biggest one first. Twain

The human race has one really effective weapon, and that is laughter. Twain

What other words come to mind with this word:

_____
_____
_____
_____
_____
_____
_____
_____
_____
_____
_____
_____
_____
_____
_____
_____
_____
_____

This is the second stage: The Adventure.

It launches when your feet touch the ground in your host country. This will be an exciting and busy time. You will be "crowded" and your daily schedule filled with new experiences. This is the time you will have to be intentional with finding a time to slip away and be alone. During this time: Listen. Read. Think. Pray. Record.

List the information you know about the country, the people, and the circumstances as you expect them to be. Later you can reflect back and compare your responses to these same questions.

Country facts:

People and culture:

Briefly describe the project and what you will be doing:

Date: _____ Word: Energy

Reading: It ain't those parts of the Bible that I can't understand that bother me, it is the parts that I do understand. Twain

How precious to me are your thoughts, O God! How vast is the sum of them! If I would count them, they are more than the sand. I awake and I am still with you. Psalm 139:17-18

What other words come to mind with this word:

_____
_____
_____
_____
_____
_____
_____
_____
_____
_____
_____
_____
_____
_____
_____
_____
_____
_____

Date: _____ Word: Abide

Reading: The value of a man should be seen in what he gives and not in what he is able to receive. Einstein.

So in everything, do to others what you would have them do to you, for this sums up the Law and the Prophets. Matthew 7:12

What other words come to mind with this word:

_____
_____
_____
_____
_____
_____
_____
_____
_____
_____
_____
_____
_____
_____
_____
_____
_____
_____
_____
_____

Date: _____ Word: Presence

Reading: There are people in the world so hungry, that God cannot appear to them except in the form of bread. Gandhi

Finally, brothers and sisters, whatever is true, whatever is noble, whatever is right, whatever is pure, whatever is lovely, whatever is admirable—if anything is excellent or praiseworthy, think about such things...And the God of peace will be with you. Philippians 4:8-9

What other words come to mind with this word:

_____
_____
_____
_____
_____
_____
_____
_____
_____
_____
_____
_____
_____
_____
_____
_____
_____
_____

Date: _____ Word: Gifted

Reading: The best way to find yourself is to lose yourself in the service to others. Gandhi

I am not saying these things because I am in need, for I have learned to be content whatever the circumstances. I know what it is to be in need, and I know what it is to have plenty. I have learned the secret of being content in any and every situation, whether well fed or hungry, whether living in plenty or in want. I can do all things though Christ who gives me strength. Philippians 4:11-13

What other words come to mind with this word:

_____
_____
_____
_____
_____
_____
_____
_____
_____
_____
_____
_____
_____
_____
_____
_____
_____

Date: _____   Word: Work

Reading: I like your Christ, I do not like your Christians. Your Christians are so unlike your Christ. Gandhi

For you created my inmost being; you knit me together in my mother's womb. I praise you because I am fearfully and wonderfully made; your works are wonderful, I know them full well. Psalm 139:13-14

What other words come to mind with this word:

_____
_____
_____
_____
_____
_____
_____
_____
_____
_____
_____
_____
_____
_____
_____
_____
_____
_____
_____

Date: _____ Word: Visible

Reading: To give pleasure to a single heart by a single act is better than a thousand heads bowing in prayer. Gandhi

Where can I go from your Spirit? Where can I flee from your presence? If I go up to the heavens, you are there; if I make my bed in the depths, you are there. If I rise on the wings of the dawn, if I settle on the far side of the sea, even there your hand will guide me, your right hand will hold me fast. Psalm 139:7-10

What other words come to mind with this word:

_____
_____
_____
_____
_____
_____
_____
_____
_____
_____
_____
_____
_____
_____
_____
_____

Date: _____ Word: Flexible

Reading: Do not store up for yourselves treasures on earth, where moths and vermin can destroy, and where thieves break in and steal. But store up for yourselves in heaven, where moths and vermin do not destroy, and where thieves do not break in and steal. For where your treasure is, there will be your heart also. Matthew 6:19-21

What other words come to mind with this word:

_____
_____
_____
_____
_____
_____
_____
_____
_____
_____
_____
_____
_____
_____
_____
_____
_____
_____
_____

Date: _____ Word: Family

Reading: I am only one, but still I am one. I cannot do everything, but still I can something; and because I cannot do everything, I will not refuse to do something I can do. Helen Keller

And Jesus grew in wisdom and stature, and in favor with God and man. Luke 2:52

What other words come to mind with this word:

_____
_____
_____
_____
_____
_____
_____
_____
_____
_____
_____
_____
_____
_____
_____
_____
_____
_____
_____
_____

Date: _____ Word: Patient

Reading: Although the world is full of suffering, it is full of the overcoming of it. Helen Keller

Come to me, all you who are weary and burdened, and I will give you rest. Take my yoke upon you and learn from me, for I am gentle and humble in heart, and you will find rest for your souls. For my yoke is easy and my burden is light. Matthew 11:28-30

What other words come to mind with this word:

_____
_____
_____
_____
_____
_____
_____
_____
_____
_____
_____
_____
_____
_____
_____
_____
_____

Date: _____   Word: Strange

Reading: Walking with a friend in the dark is better than walking alone in the light. Helen Keller

Jesus stood up and cried out, "If anyone thirsts, let him come to me and drink." John 7:37

What other words come to mind with this word:

_____

_____

_____

_____

_____

_____

_____

_____

_____

_____

_____

_____

_____

_____

_____

_____

_____

_____

_____

_____

_____

_____

Date: _____ Word: Weakness

Reading: You must be the change you wish to see in the world. Gandhi

And he said to them, "You shall love the Lord your God with all your heart, and with all your soul, and with all your mind. This is the great and first commandment. And a second is like it, You shall love your neighbor as yourself. On these two commandments depend all the Law and the Prophets. Matthew 22:37-40

What other words come to mind with this word:

_____
_____
_____
_____
_____
_____
_____
_____
_____
_____
_____
_____
_____
_____
_____
_____
_____
_____

Date: _____   Word: Sick

Reading: When I admire the wonders of a sunset or the beauty of the moon, my soul expands in the worship of the creator. Gandhi

The heavens declare to glory of God and the sky above proclaims his handiwork. Psalm 19:1

What other words come to mind with this word:

_____
_____
_____
_____
_____
_____
_____
_____
_____
_____
_____
_____
_____
_____
_____
_____
_____
_____
_____

Date: _____ Word: Beginning

Reading: A religion that takes no account of practical affairs and does not help to solve them is no religion. Gandhi

What other words come to mind with this word:

_____
_____
_____
_____
_____
_____
_____
_____
_____
_____
_____
_____
_____
_____
_____
_____
_____
_____
_____
_____
_____

The third stage is the post-Adventure.

It begins when your feet touch the ground in your home country. There will be memories. Enthusiasm from what you have just experienced. A gradual return to your normal routine. You will go through shifting emotions and begin to merge your recent Adventure with the normal routines of being home. This is a critical time to capture what is passing through your mind and heart. During this stage: Listen. Read. Think. Pray. Record.

Write one-word sentences that capture the images of your Adventure.

_____

_____

_____

Is there one thing that stands out, is louder than any other?

_____

_____

_____

What has changed?

_____

_____

_____

Is there anything that brings sadness to your heart?

_____

_____

_____

As we re-enter your normal world there are five phases of emotional adjustment that are common after an international experience. Use this to as to reflect upon during the following days and weeks.

5 Possible Stages for Re-entry

The following chart illustrates the cycle you may go through emotionally as you re-enter your home world.

Have Fun (honeymoon). Sharing the stories. Re-living the adventure.

Flee (avoidance). May begin to feel alone. Most of your family and friends have not had this adventure and cannot relate to what you have gone through and what you are feeling.

Fight (anger, criticism). Emotionally begin to fight back. Feelings of how unfair our way of life is compare to what you have just experienced. Anger at others not understanding.

Fit In (tolerance of differences). Survival. Acceptance and willing to acknowledge that others cannot know and experience what you feel. And acceptance of idea that only when you experience first-hand will understanding surface of what goes on in third world countries.

Be Fruitful (creative engagement). Finding ways to encourage others to share this same adventure you have had. Educating others and challenging others on the needs of the world, both spiritual needs and physical needs.

(Adapted from Lisa Espineli Chinn, Reentry Guide for Short TermMission Leaders, *Orlando: DeeperRoots Publications p. 14, used by permission of the author.)*

Date: _____ Word: Change

Reading: Everyman dies. But not everyman lives. Braveheart.

The tongue has the power of life and death, and those who love it will eat its fruit. Proverbs 18:21

What other words come to mind with this word:

_____
_____
_____
_____
_____
_____
_____
_____
_____
_____
_____
_____
_____
_____
_____
_____
_____
_____
_____
_____
_____
_____
_____

Date: _____ Word: Direction

Reading: The best way to cheer yourself up is to try to cheer somebody else up. Twain

The generous will themselves be blessed, for they share food with the poor. Proverbs 22

What other words come to mind with this word:

_____
_____
_____
_____
_____
_____
_____
_____
_____
_____
_____
_____
_____
_____
_____
_____
_____
_____
_____
_____
_____

Date: _____ Word: Seed

Reading: Don't let schooling interfere with your education. Twain

Ask and it will be given to you; seek and you will find; knock and the door will be opened to you. For everyone who asks receives; the one who seeks finds; and the one who knocks, the door will be opened. Matthew 7:7-8

What other words come to mind with this word:

_____
_____
_____
_____
_____
_____
_____
_____
_____
_____
_____
_____
_____
_____
_____
_____
_____
_____
_____

Date: _____ Word: Rugged

Reading: I long to accomplish a great and noble task, but it is my chief duty to accomplish small tasks as if they were great and noble. Helen Keller

By the seventh day God had finished the work he had been doing; so on the seventh day he rested from all his work. Genesis 2:2

What other words come to mind with this word:

_____
_____
_____
_____
_____
_____
_____
_____
_____
_____
_____
_____
_____
_____
_____
_____
_____
_____
_____
_____

Date: _____ Word: Quiet

Reading: Alone we can do so little; together we can do so much. Helen Keller

What other words come to mind with this word:

_____
_____
_____
_____
_____
_____
_____
_____
_____
_____
_____
_____
_____
_____
_____
_____
_____
_____
_____
_____
_____
_____

Date: _____   Word: Adventure

Reading: The most important thing in communication is hearing what isn't said. Peter Drucker

Take note of this: Everyone should be quick to listen, slow to speak, and slow to become angry. James 1:19

What other words come to mind with this word:

_____

_____

_____

_____

_____

_____

_____

_____

_____

_____

_____

_____

_____

_____

_____

_____

_____

_____

_____

_____

_____

Date: _____ Word: Time

Reading: If we are to go forward, we must go back and rediscover those precious values—that all reality hinges on moral foundations and that all reality has spiritual control. Martin Luther King, Jr.

Trust in the Lord with all your heart and lean not on your own understanding; in all your ways acknowledge him, and he will make straight your paths. Proverbs 3:5-6

What other words come to mind with this word:

_____
_____
_____
_____
_____
_____
_____
_____
_____
_____
_____
_____
_____
_____
_____
_____
_____
_____

Date: _____   Word: Home

Reading: I have a dream that my four children will one day live in a nation where they will not be judged by the color of their skin, but by the content of their character. Martin Luther King, Jr.

Above all else, guard your heart, for everything you do flows from it. Proverbs 4:23

What other words come to mind with this word:

_____
_____
_____
_____
_____
_____
_____
_____
_____
_____
_____
_____
_____
_____
_____
_____
_____
_____
_____

Date: _____ Word: Health

Reading: Prayer is not an old woman's idle amusement. Properly understood and applied, it is the most potent instrument of action. Gandhi

What other words come to mind with this word:

_____
_____
_____
_____
_____
_____
_____
_____
_____
_____
_____
_____
_____
_____
_____
_____
_____
_____
_____
_____
_____
_____

Date: _____ Word: Field

Reading: The pursuit of truth and beauty is a sphere of activity in which we are permitted to remain children all of our lives. Einstein

Jesus answered, I am the way and the truth and the life. John 14:6

What other words come to mind with this word:

_____
_____
_____
_____
_____
_____
_____
_____
_____
_____
_____
_____
_____
_____
_____
_____
_____
_____
_____

About Wine to Water

Wine to Water's US staff consists of six full-time and five part-time members. We consider ourselves family but live in different parts of the country and are seldom in the same place at once. We are united by our passion for clean water and the joy we get from working with our local partners on the ground. Wine To Water has worked in 17 countries. We have ongoing projects in eight countries on four continents, and support thirty international aid workers.

How We Began

Wine To Water was a dream that became a reality in early 2004. We held our first fundraiser in Raleigh, North Carolina in February of 2004. Originally, the concept was to put on benefit wine events then use the money raised to support water projects around the world. The first fundraiser was a great success. Other events followed and we gained confidence that Wine to Water would grow as an organization. Wine tastings have become one of many ways that we raise awareness and support for the global water crisis. We have provided clean water and sanitation to over 250,000 people in 17 countries to date.

Our Name

The first miracle Jesus performed was turning water into wine. He was at a wedding that ran out of wine early in the evening, threatening to end the celebration. Jesus asked the servants to fill stone jugs with water. He then transformed the water into wine. This miraculous but simple gift allowed the small community to keep celebrating. Wine to water strives to expand our global community by providing those who are fortunate an opportunity to give the gift of clean water. John 2:9-10